WHO
CARES?

McCourtney Institute for Democracy

The Pennsylvania State University's McCourtney Institute for Democracy (http://democracyinstitute.la.psu.edu) was founded in 2012 as an interdisciplinary center for research, teaching, and outreach on democracy. The institute coordinates innovative programs and projects in collaboration with the Center for American Political Responsiveness and the Center for Democratic Deliberation.

Laurence and Lynne Brown Democracy Medal

The Laurence and Lynne Brown Democracy Medal recognizes outstanding individuals, groups, and organizations that produce exceptional innovations to further democracy in the United States or around the world. In even numbered years, the medal spotlights practical innovations, such as new institutions, laws, technologies, or movements that advance the cause of democracy. Awards given in odd numbered years highlight advances in democratic theory that enrich philosophical conceptions of democracy or empirical models of democratic behavior, institutions, or systems.

WHO CARES?

HOW TO RESHAPE
A DEMOCRATIC POLITICS

JOAN C. TRONTO

CORNELL SELECTS
An imprint of
CORNELL UNIVERSITY PRESS
Ithaca and London

Cornell Selects, *an imprint of Cornell University Press, provides a forum for advancing provocative ideas and fresh viewpoints through outstanding digital and print publications. Longer than an article and shorter than a book, titles published under this imprint explore a diverse range of topics in a clear and concise format—one designed to appeal to any reader. Cornell Selects publications continue the Press's long tradition of supporting high quality scholarship and sharing it with the wider community, promoting a culture of broad inquiry that is a vital aspect of the mission of Cornell University.*

First published 2015 by Cornell University Press
First printing, Cornell Paperbacks, 2015

Printed in the United States of America

Library of Congress Cataloging-in-Publication Data

Tronto, Joan C., 1952–
    Who cares? : How to reshape a democratic politics / Joan C. Tronto.
        pages cm
    Includes bibliographical references and index.
    ISBN 978-1-5017-0274-7 (pbk. : alk. paper)
1. Social medicine. 2. Medical policy. 3. Caregivers. I. Title.
    RA418.T735 2016
    362.1—dc23   2015031018

Cornell University Press strives to use environmentally responsible suppliers and materials to the fullest extent possible in the publishing of its books. Such materials include vegetable-based, low-VOC inks and acid-free papers that are recycled, totally chlorine-free, or partly composed of nonwood fibers. For further information, visit our website at www.cornellpress.cornell.edu.

Paperback printing   10 9 8 7 6 5 4 3 2 1

Contents

Acknowledgments

I have written this essay on the occasion of receiving the Brown Democracy Medal from Penn State University. The medal, presented annually by the McCourtney Institute for Democracy in Penn State's College of the Liberal Arts, was endowed by Larry and Lynne Brown, Class of 1971 (history) and Class of 1972 (education) respectively, to spotlight ideas to improve democracy in the United States and around the world. I am deeply honored to receive the Brown Medal this year, and I am grateful to the Browns for endowing the medal and to the McCourtney Institute for Democracy at Penn State for administering it. John Gastil, the director of the Institute, and editor Sarah Cypher also provided invaluable editorial advice and support in writing this essay. I also want to acknowledge Raymond Duvall of the University of Minnesota, Mary Dietz of Northwestern University for supporting my application for the award, and Jim Stanger of

Channel Z in Minneapolis for his assistance in preparing the application.

Over the past thirty years or so, I have discussed care as an ethical and political ideal with countless scholars, students, activists, and care practitioners, and I am grateful to all for what I have learned from this growing "care ethics" community. Berenice Fisher and I devised the original definition of caring that has served as the foundation for all of my subsequent work, and I remain in her debt. My students, often skeptical about these ideas, have provided valuable assistance. And my life would not be as rich as it is without all of the family members, friends, and colleagues with whom I share and care. I am also grateful to NYU Press for publishing *Caring Democracy: Markets, Equality, and Justice* (2013).

Finally, I draw inspiration every day from seeing so much caring and democratic energy all around me. From protests around "Black Lives Matter" to support for food banks, citizens are pressing our democracy to become more caring. To care well and to orient our daily concerns to improve the prospect of democratic life often require heroic daily efforts. I hope this essay calls attention to an existing reality of ongoing care and commitments to equality that I see every day. And I hope it inspires others to help to transform our current politics to make democratic caring into a central value.

WHO CARES?

Introduction

Usually we think of the worlds of care and of politics as far apart. This is partly because we wrongly think that care is all about compassion and kindness, and that politics is all about one-upmanship. Indeed, what world seems less caring than the rough-and-tumble one of backstabbing competition that we think of as politics? This way of thinking has a long pedigree in political thought; even Aristotle believed that first you are cared for, and then you are ready to enter politics. To Aristotle, caring is a realm of unequal relations irrelevant to wielding power as a political actor.

But there is another way to think about the link between care and politics. These two worlds are deeply intertwined, and even more so in a democracy. Only at the expense of our democracy do we underestimate their interdependence. And we need to rethink this relationship if democracy is to continue.

We hear often that we are in a care crisis. That is, we face a shortage of formal caregivers to cope with the increased care needs of ever-more elders who will need ever-more care. But this crisis involves more than demographic and labor market projections. We all experience a version of it daily: "I wish I had more time: to care for my loved ones, to contribute to causes I care about, to be there for my friends." We spend so much time on undesirable tasks and so little time on ones we really value. How can everything be so upside down? This pressure seems to each of us a personal failing. But it isn't. It's a *political* problem. I will argue that what ails our democracy is not (or not only) that there is too much money in politics, or that elections aren't meaningful or deliberative enough, or that there are myriad other concerns about how we conduct our democratic politics. Instead, I want to argue that what we currently call "politics" is wrong, and that our obsession with market-foremost democracy distorts what should be the most fundamental concern: care. The market can't make ethical decisions about who receives what care, yet we've organized our democracy to leave large segments of the polity priced out of the markets that would make us better when we are ill, educate us when we are ready to learn, let us spend time with our children if we have them, and ensure the safety of our loved ones. The result is disastrous for the kind of equality that is essential to a functioning democracy. Fixing it requires a new understanding of care and a better definition of democracy.

When We Understand Care, We'll Need to Redefine Democracy

Defining Care

When I say "care," I don't mean only healthcare, childcare, and caring for the elderly. I don't mean only finding a babysitter on a website called Care.com. I mean, as Berenice Fisher and I defined it some time ago, "in the most general sense, care is a species activity that includes everything we do to maintain, continue, and repair our world so that we may live in it as well as possible. That world includes our bodies, our selves, and our environment, all of which we seek to interweave in a complex, life-sustaining web."[1]

Usually, when people hear this definition, they are a little stunned. It is *so* broad; it seems as if almost everything we do touches upon care. This is true: care shows up everywhere in our lives. Now, we don't usually think of care on this broad and most general level. Particular care practices— for example, performing brain surgery, teaching middle school, detailing a car—all have different, defining elements.

What they have in common, though, is an effort to keep their corners of the world going by doing laundry, planning the financial support of an intellectually disabled adult, preparing children's lunches, and so forth. Care is about meeting needs, and it is always *relational*: the skinned knee of a child who fell off his bike isn't only about scrapes and germs, it is also about creating the conditions for him to feel safe in the world.

Not everyone agrees on the best ways to give or receive care. The standard, "so that we may live in the world as well as possible," is very flexible. In some caring practices, the requirements are clear. Physicians and engineers are obliged to meet a standard of care that accords with the best scientific evidence. Yet at a more general level, the standards of care accord with society's values. And these change; what was corporal punishment a generation ago is more often called child abuse now.

If we believe that moral and political issues should have straightforward, principled answers, there is another feature of caring that will seem frustrating. To make caring well a central moral concern presupposes a different kind of moral and political theory because it doesn't begin from abstract principles and reason down to pronouncements about what is right and wrong. It starts in the middle of things. Care practices don't suddenly begin; they are already ongoing. Just as in democracy, there are always disagreements, messy distractions, and complications. The trick is to determine the best ways of caring in a particular time and situation. And this depends on establishing a democratic process of assessing and meeting care needs.

So, then, what does it mean to care well? Often we think of care as just some extra put into a task—for example, a more caring nurse makes a point of conversing with his patients before bedtime. But we can and must be more explicit about what constitutes good caring. As a starting place for reimagining democracy along caring lines, Berenice Fisher and I devised four phases of care that help us analyze care practices more fully. We noted that caring well occurs when these different parts fit together.

1. *Caring about.* First, care proceeds from meeting needs. While some needs seem obvious, discerning a need is actually a complicated task. Even simple examples belie this complexity. The baby is crying: Does it need a bottle? Simply to be held? Most examples are much more complex. The people "on the other side of the tracks" are poor: Why? Such questions invite complex thinking about "the politics of needs interpretation."[2] In the first place, then, care requires caring about: identifying caring needs.

2. *Caring for.* Second, just because a need exists does not mean that anyone in particular has to address it. In cities, people often walk by the homeless as if they weren't there, perhaps thinking, "Somebody should do something about

that . . ." Accepting responsibility and realizing that something has to be done is the second phase of care.

3. *Caregiving.* Once a need is identified and someone has taken responsibility for addressing it, meeting it requires work. The third phase of care is the actual task of caregiving. The epidemiologists need to study how the virus spreads, the floodwaters need to be dammed, someone needs to teach the new students English, and so on. Most caregiving raises questions about good care practices. Do vouchers for food work better than giving people surplus cheese? Does being a stern teacher help students or push them too hard? Is the faucet leak fixed? And here is another complication: The people who recognize the need are not necessarily the same ones who take responsibility for fixing it, and those responsible are not necessarily those who do the actual caregiving. A son might be responsible for arranging his parents' doctor visits from another city, so he calls his father's social worker. But if those who are responsible allocate resources based on a too-limited scope of caring, then they may allocate too little. It's a frequent problem—hospitals often have insufficient supplies; for example, of telemetry units. Caregivers learn to cope with caring in less-than-ideal circumstances.

4. *Care-receiving.* After the work of caring is done, another phase remains. How do we know the care was successful?

Care-receiving prompts a response. Given how pervasive care is, some of it is routine: washing the dishes after dinner, filling potholes in the spring, etc. But even if care-receivers do not say "Thank you, that helped"—for neither the baby nor the patient still in a coma will necessarily do so—care is not complete until the need is met. That requires looking again at the situation and the resources assigned to improve it. And, often, looking again will lead to recognizing new needs, and the process repeats. Endlessly. Needs never end until we die. Care is always present, rarely visible, always requiring something from us.

As you might expect, caring involves moral and value commitments. Each phase of care can be tied to specific moral practices, and indeed might be a basis for how our democracy imagines a "good citizen." Because we become better at things as we do them more, care practices deepen certain moral and daily skills. That is what a practice means. Therefore, "caring about" makes us *attentive*. When we have to be on the lookout for unmet needs, we begin to notice needs more. People who work in women's shelters are more likely to spot abuse victims elsewhere because these workers are attentive to this type of problem. Next, "caring for" makes us *responsible*. Taking on responsibilities trains our eye to notice when responsibilities have and have not been taken on by others. It becomes second nature for elementary school teachers to ask, "Who is going to volunteer for the cleanup committee?" because they always think about responsibility among their students. Caregiving also makes us *competent*. If we are expected to monitor a patient's blood pressure, then we need to know how to do it. Competence is not simply a technical measure; for most people, it becomes a measure of their excellence. Finally, care-receiving makes us *responsive*. If we are going to measure the effects of our care, then we need to know what has happened, how the cared-for people or things responded to this care, and what we might do next. In a democratic setting, we will want to ask care-receivers to respond, if they can, to the quality of the care they were given. And in their response, we are likely to hear the articulation of new needs that must then be addressed.

So, care is a complex process, and it also shapes what we pay attention to, how we think about responsibility, what we do, how responsive we are to the world around us, and what we think of as important in life. In short, a functioning democracy is full of people who are attentive, responsible, competent, and responsive.

Care is already everywhere. And we all are not only givers of care, we are also—each and every one of us—receivers of care. This is true of all humans when they are young, old, or infirm. But it is also true of you and me every day. Each day, we arrange to feed, clothe, and surround ourselves so that we may live in the world as well as possible. We care for others and for ourselves, and others care for us. We stop by the grocery store and buy prepared food for dinner and expect the trash to be picked up. All of this caring activity is constantly going on around us. It is so ever-present that we rarely think about it. But now that we have begun to think about it here, let's notice something else about it. Care is always infused with power. And this makes care deeply political.

Care and Politics

S aying that care is deeply political requires us to think of politics with both a small "p" and a capital "P." Small-p politics occurs in everyday life. We don't usually think of our many daily interactions as political, but I argue that we should. Everyday life is political because all caring, every response to a need, involves power relationships. Especially when we are thinking about the care that we can't provide for ourselves, caregivers are in a position of relative power. Infants are at the mercy of their caregivers for protection and food, and sometimes caregivers wield that power in tragic ways. Doctors have power over their patients, and hospitals have worked out protocols (such as informed consent) to try to protect us from abuses of such power.

Furthermore, every caring need can be met in myriad ways. How do we respond to the resident in the nursing home who screams "Help me!" all night? Working out a solution with the caregivers, the family, the resident, and other residents is a political process. All of this caring requires "politics" in the sense that actors with unequal power come together to determine an outcome.

But let's pull back a bit further and we'll see that capital-P Politics is also at work here. Every caring act occurs in a larger political context that reflects a given society's values, laws, customs, and institutions. Let's return to the screaming nursing home resident. Why is that elderly man there in the first place? Decisions have been made: individually by the resident and his family, socially through a set of values about where and how old people should live, and legally and politically by provision of Medicare, Medicaid, and regulations to control how nursing homes get paid. On the broadest level, all societies organize care activities.

As a result, thinking about Political solutions to a single care problem necessarily ripples outward, with consequences for democracy. Consider this familiar example: Parents with children in school are keenly aware that academic schedules and work schedules do not line up. School days are shorter than workdays, and children are home all summer. For school-age kids, the hours between the end of school and when their parents get home are the most precarious, when kids are most likely to get into trouble. For less-well-off parents, with less access to affordable childcare, these discrepancies are even worse. Suppose that, as democratic citizens, we could figure out how to fix the school calendar issue. School might begin before parents had to be at work, and end an hour after parents leave work. School vacations might align with work vacations. But how could we do that, given the demands of work? Well, we would have to think long and hard about who should work when. Perhaps work hours should be adjusted over the course of one's life— parents could take those hours now and work harder when their children are grown. Childless people could bank their extra hours and retire earlier. The possibilities are broad. But to fix this one thing would require fundamental changes to our society's organization of time. And once we start to think about it, we need to reorder not only school schedules but school curricula. Work schedules would need to be adapted. Transportation would need to be reorganized. Indeed, we might want to rethink what kinds of housing parents live in: Does it make sense to live in suburban sprawl if the goal is to organize life around getting children easily to and from school? How much should such matters be controlled and organized on a local level? A state level? A national level?

We might feel that care is natural, but as soon as we remember that care depends upon how we wish to live in the world "as well as possible," care no longer appears to be an instinctual process. When we look closely, we see difficult Politics again. Not even childrearing is exempt. How should babies be named, and by whom? Should they have their ears pierced early, and should little boys be circumcised? Care practices beg decisions about who does what, and illuminate that caring is not only Political (happening at the institutional level), but political, occurring in everyday life and decisions.

Some societies mark certain people as slaves or as members of a lower caste, relegating the dirty work to them. Some societies declare that care occurs in the household and is not a concern in public life. There are countless ways for societies to organize caring. No society could exist, though, without customs, traditions, laws, and regulations of caring practices. Every society also has, then, a culture of care that is congruent with its social and political institutions and its broader culture and practices.

Throughout most of human history, in most human societies, caring has been associated with lowly people. Childcare workers are among the lowest-paid workers in the United States. Those who provide non-nurturant, "dirty work" care are the least well-regarded in society.[3] Again, this point seems natural to us: the aristocrats of *Downton Abbey* have a retinue of servants, as we'd expect among the affluent of their place and time. Being powerful means that you have someone else caring for you. Care is not only about the happy moments of saving a patient's life, watching a student have a "light bulb" moment, or receiving a caress of gratitude from a loved one. Care is also about drudgery—difficult, conflicting work. What it means to be powerful, in caring terms, is to be able to foist off the unpleasant parts of care onto others and to take on only the care duties we find worthwhile.

But if citizens boost their self-importance by making others care for them, and exercise their power to avoid drudgery, then how does care shake out in a society that is, in principle, committed to the idea that everyone is equal? If all societies have to organize care in some way, then is there a more democratic way to care?

Historically, democracies have opted to leave some people outside of political life and assign caregiving duties to them. Ancient Athenian democracy, which we often regard as a highly participatory democracy, restricted political roles to those who could be considered equal; that is, men who were born into citizenship. Women, slaves, children, and metics (workers whose families at some point came from abroad) were excluded from being citizens because, among other things, they had "domestic duties."[4] As modern democracies have struggled to become more inclusive, they have had to rethink an easy formula: "Let's assign care work to those we have excluded from full citizenship."[5] Because care is so ubiquitous, and our questions about equality are so much at the center of social values, it might be best to think about democracy in terms of organizing care. By this account, we can redefine democracy to capture the way it has to manage care.

So, here you might notice a paradox at the crux of my proposition. Democracy requires that people be equal, but mainly, care is about inequality. How can we think about turning something that is so unequal into something that is equal?

Caring With

Any given act of care is unequal. But across generations, and across any given person's lifetime, we can set a democratic goal to even out these inequalities. Recipients of Medicare are not called sponges or freeloaders; they are called "senior citizens" because Medicare and Social Security are an acknowledgment of their past caring contributions. Throughout our lives, there are times of particular need and particular abundance. This balancing of care roles can thus occur on a social level. We can even call it a fifth phase of care: *caring with*. The first four phases of care imagined a citizen as someone who is attentive, responsible, competent, and responsive; "caring with" imagines the entire polity of citizens engaged in a lifetime of commitment to and benefiting from these principles. "Caring with" is our new democratic ideal.

What makes care equal is not the perfection of an individual caring act, but that we can trust that over time, we will be able to reciprocate the care we received from fellow citizens, and that they will reciprocate the care we've given to them. In such an ongoing pattern of care, we can expect moral virtues to deepen: We will trust in one another and in our social and political institutions, and feel solidarity with other citizens, seeing them as partners in our own caregiving and receiving. Life being what it is, we shouldn't expect everything to come out exactly "even Steven" in the end. But our goal as democratic citizens is to guarantee that huge imbalances are rectified. Our political processes shoul ensure that everyone can express grievances. If some people are still doing too much of the "dirty work" of caring, then they can be heard. What we'll equalize, then, are not acts of caregiving, but responsibilities for care—and as a prerequisite, the discussions about how those responsibilities are being allocated. Hence, we arrive at a new definition of democracy: *Democracy is the allocation of caring responsibilities and assuring that everyone can participate in those allocations of care as completely as possible.*[6]

But here you might object. Don't we do that already? Isn't the United States a progressive nation? The goal of a "caring-with" democracy is not to assume that when we say "all men are created equal," we mean all people *are* always, exactly equal. This problem has been solved in most democratic theory by assuming that we are equal enough. Yet when we think about a random citizen, the sometimes-mistaken picture in our heads is of someone who possesses full rationality and acts only on reason in making decisions about their lives.

This picture limits democratic inclusion, however, to only some aspects of a human being. When people are vulnerable, needy, or responding to an emotional impetus, they somehow slip beyond our assumptions about what defines a "citizen." Perhaps our aspiration should be not only to think of ourselves as citizens in those moments of perfect adulthood, but to acknowledge that we are citizens throughout our lives. If we broadened our general image of a citizen to truly include all citizens, then we would broaden how we think about ourselves and others. We often presume that people are exactly like us (and should act as we do), or that they are somehow deeply "other." But a new caring vision would recognize everyone—young, old, infirm, and other—as part of an ongoing system of caring acts in which we're sometimes on an extreme end of the giving–receiving scale, and sometimes in the middle. Equality is not a starting point for democratic citizens. It is something that all citizens achieve, not through an "identity" as citizen, but through concerted action over a lifetime. If democratic citizenship is to be truly inclusive, then we have to recognize that caring is what will get us there together.

We, as citizens, need to decide in general terms how caring will be organized. Not everyone needs to do all of the caring work, nor do all the details about caring need to be organized by government. But the general handing-out of care responsibilities is a political question, and one we should address through politics.

Furthermore, because exclusion has often been the way in which some are stuck with disproportionate caring responsibilities, it is important that everyone be included in this process. Otherwise, historically, those who are excluded will remain stuck with such duties. Let's explore what that means by holding a mirror up to the state of care—and democracy—in the United States today.

Care, Inc.

A Free Market for All?

Usually, when we think of democracy, we think of it as a set of institutional arrangements by which we choose officeholders. When we try to think about why we choose officeholders democratically (that is, what officeholders should try to achieve), we simply say that they should try to maximize liberty and equality for citizens. Increasingly, however, democratic politics has come to be about managing the economy, which resurrects the question: To what end?

The most common answer provided in the United States today is that the purpose of managing the economy is to allow the market to have the freest reign. This presumes that a free market yields free democratic citizens. From the standpoint of care, however, this way of thinking is deeply flawed. There's a deep connection between Politics as national policy and the politics of everyday life. Institutions shape who we are and how we think of ourselves as citizens. If we wish to create the conditions for citizens to be equally free to care as they wish for themselves and others, then we need to rethink this market-foremost orientation.

For most of American history, care was done in households. With the growth of industrialization and urbanization, more work and more care became separated from the household. Certain tasks that had been organized around the household and around local institutions such as churches (for example, tasks dealing with birth, death, education, and provision of clothing and shelter) moved outside the home and became professionalized. Some forms of this care became the government's responsibility—taking on public education, creating police departments, keeping vital statistics on births, deaths, marriages, and so forth. Other care services were moved outside of the home and into the marketplace.

Our current model of caring depends on the household, the market, and the state. As households became smaller, more care became professionalized on the market. From ready-to-wear clothing to packaged flour or cough syrup to nannies for hire, receiving care depends on having money. Earning wages is the way to acquire money, allowing household goods to be bought and then converted, through the efforts of those in the household, into household care.[7] Early in the twentieth century, reformers argued for a "family wage"—a minimum wage set high enough to maintain an entire household on one worker's salary.[8] Through such mechanisms as minimum wage laws, government indirectly ensured that households would be able to do the caring work that they needed to do. The government has also managed direct allocations of care, for example, in the creation of Social Security in the 1930s, Medicare in the 1960s, and the Affordable Care Act in the 2000s. Today, however, in part because current ideology holds that markets are better than governments, most care is organized through the market.

The Market-Foremost Democracy

As our democracy has become more attuned to the needs of inclusiveness, old values have been displaced by attitudes of greater equality. As a result, care has changed over time. Gender still predicts who does most of the professional care work in society, and race and socioeconomic background still predict who is most likely to get stuck doing the dirty work of care.[9] This persists even if we no longer believe that women or people of color are uniquely suited for caring professions.

Yet there is another side to this greater openness. We have fallen into a vicious circle of thinking about care primarily from the standpoint of market-foremost democracy. Market-foremost care operates within an economic order often called neoliberalism. This "liberalism" refers not to the left wing of the Democratic Party in the United States, but to the historical association of the free market of capitalism with political freedom, which is usually associated with democracy. In the classical account, if government interferes with the market, it reduces people's freedom. In the neoliberal model, these concerns have been updated to take into consideration the roles that governments have come to play in helping citizens care for themselves, and the increasingly global nature of the market. Thus, neoliberals argue against trade restrictions, and they favor the defunding of state-run institutions such as public schools. Neoliberals go further and describe how people must conduct themselves to fit into this new economic order.[10] Neoliberalism affects not just Politics, but politics on a cultural scale.

Some refer to this change as the Reagan Revolution. "Government is not the solution," President Reagan said, "it is the problem." Far from a partisan quip, this view has dominated our political culture for a generation. Bill Clinton and every president since have repeated the mantra, "The era of big government is over."

The main steps of this argument, reconstructed, go something like this: The market is the most efficient way to allocate goods and services, and since the market has become global, the world has become "flat."[11] Global competition requires you to reshape your attitude; you can't be coddled, and you have to face tough new realities. Businesses need to be free from labor restrictions in order to be flexible. Everything needs to be calculated to maximize profit. "Accountability" for schools means that there have to be measurable and reliable outcomes that we can use to compare them, one to another. Competition keeps people on their toes, so if you worry that you will lose your job, then you should work harder. To this market system, British prime minister Margaret Thatcher explained, "there is no alternative."

But, of course, there are other ways to organize a political economy. Consider the question of job creation. To create more jobs, politicians promise tax breaks to a local business if it builds a plant in Town A. But Town B enters the ring, offering longer-term tax breaks. Town B wins and gets the jobs, but it loses future tax revenue. In the past, however, a leading way to create jobs was simply to raise taxes and have the government hire people. As John Maynard Keynes argued, with the "multiplier effect" that wages have in a community, the result is a stronger economy. This was the favored economic solution in the mid-twentieth century. It is all the more amazing, then, that we have so quickly assumed that Thatcher is right—that there is no alternative to the market-driven system.

Criticisms and defenses can be made of these economic policies, and I don't intend to explicate all of these arguments. My point is simply that the effect of market-foremost democracy on caring is clear: it creates great inequalities and diminishes the sense of "caring with."

The Market-Foremost Citizen

Neoliberal economic changes have created small-p political changes as well. First, Americans are spending more of their time at work. The middle-class family now needs close to two good salaries to get by; a "family wage" is rare. As a result, parents work harder. They spend time with their kids differently, trying to squeeze "quality time" out of every interaction. "Making memories" requires spending money on vacations. Some say children are becoming less skilled in daily living,[12] but they do learn to be consummate consumers—because their parents, feeling guilty, buy them more, and because they are increasingly "born to shop."[13] The other side of the market, after all, is that one needs people to buy an endless number of goods.

As wealth increasingly resembles a pyramid, the logic of "winner takes all" economics becomes more firmly rooted.[14] In these circumstances, what it means to be a good parent is to ensure that your child has greater advantages than other children. The assumption is that the best schools should be for those who are best able to take advantage of the opportunity; to admit lesser students would "waste" the opportunities. Parenting becomes competitive. In such a situation, what incentive can there be for paying more to make other children's bad schools better? In a way, affluent families benefit if other children's schools are inferior. In this wide-open market, care can only mean "care for yourself and for your family."

If all of this sounds familiar, so will the myth of personal responsibility. Our market-foremost democracy frames care as an individual problem. As President George W. Bush put the point in his first inaugural address, "America, at its best, is a place where personal responsibility is valued and expected. Encouraging responsibility is not a search for scapegoats, it is a call to conscience. And though it requires sacrifice, it brings a deeper fulfillment. We find the fullness of life not only in options, but in commitments. And we find that children and community are the commitments that set us free."[15]

This is a fascinating passage. Bush's elision from responsibility to "children" and "community" makes clear that for him, personal responsibility is the solution to the problem of care in the modern state. If you can't care for your own children and your own community, the problem is your inadequate sacrifice. The opening words of the paragraph, "Encouraging responsibility is not a call for scapegoats," actually sounds as if it is indeed a call for scapegoats. Bush seems to suggest that people who are poor and not well cared for are at fault because those around them have not been sufficiently responsible for their children or communities.

Yet then the president says something that seems to contradict the logic of market-foremost caring—he invokes caring as what gives life meaning: "We find the fullness of life not only in options, but in commitments. And we find that children and community are the commitments that set us free." On the one hand, the "fullness of life" comes not only from exercising choice, but from having commitments such as raising children and caring for the community.

Bush is trying to invoke a different conception of freedom, one similar to the one I am defending here. What makes life worth living is not simply the capacity to exercise choice, but to fulfill one's hopes to care well. But this idea of freedom is still too abstract, because it presumes that we can judge other people's "personal responsibility" by the standards that govern our lives. Not everyone, however, is similarly situated, nor has the same resources to create choices for themselves.

Imagine two school children, one whose two parents are college-educated professionals earning considerable income. At home, the child has books, a place to study, and a computer with high-speed Internet. She probably has heard millions more words than her classmate.[16] The second student lives with her single mother who works two minimum-wage jobs. This mother will lose a day's salary if she takes off to visit the teacher. Which student will garner more of the teacher's attention? Even if the two kids are in the same classroom at the same school, how can we say that they have "equal opportunity?"

Yet as current policies often demonstrate, there is no context for "children" and "community" other than that of personal responsibility; as if totting up people's willingness to take on personal responsibility can predict how well children and communities will do.

Now, I am not saying people should ignore their personal responsibilities. Yet as the *only* form of responsibility, personal responsibility can have a profoundly antidemocratic effect. Taking care of one's community has a different meaning in a well-endowed, gated community than in a down-on-its-luck urban neighborhood. The market teaches us to expect that everything be on an equal and open basis. However when we act on the assumption that everyone's starting and ending points are the same, we inoculate ourselves against thinking in a broader and more caring way.

Over time, a market-foremost democracy creates an undemocratic, uncaring hierarchy among citizens. The most important resource for caring is time. Alas, time is not equally available to everyone. Professionals work many hours, but so do workers who are employed at close to the minimum wage and who hold down several jobs. Lower-paying jobs also come with fewer benefits, fewer sick days, and fewer personal days. Although the professional worker may be short on time, he has greater resources to employ in addressing his care needs.

The market, in a way, is designed for citizens such as him. Perhaps one-sixth of the paid economy is now spent on care.[17] Life coaches, dog walkers, hospital aides, chefs, teachers, wedding planners, car mechanics, and sommeliers—all are engaged in caring and sell this care on the market. And those with more economic resources are better able to buy this care (and better care); for instance, students who have tutors will likely do better on standardized tests than students who do not. In the very upper strata of the economy, high-tech firms have begun to reward their employees by providing takeout dinners, dry cleaning services, bike repair, and workout facilities on location.[18] How different are these experiences from those of the office janitor? In an era where bankruptcy looms, unequal care gives some a great advantage over others. As time and money become more unequal, care resources and care itself become more and more unequal, too.

There is an even more disturbing dimension of the market-foremost citizen. Inequality is undesirable in principle, but if some people are able to buy much of their care while the rest do most of their own care work, then we are likely to encounter a pernicious separation in the body politic. In his 1888 book, *Looking Backwards, 2000–1887*, Edward Bellamy described such an unequal society, illustrating how its citizens would perceive one another. He used the metaphor of society as a gigantic coach, in which the rich ride in relative luxury while the poor pull the coach down the road:

> *The other* fact is yet more curious, consisting in a singular hallucination which those on the top of the coach generally shared, that they were not exactly like their brothers and sisters who pulled at the rope, but of finer clay, in some way belonging to a higher order of beings who might justly expect to be drawn. . . . The strangest thing about the hallucination was that those who had but just climbed up from the ground, before they had outgrown the marks of the rope upon their hands, began to fall under its influence. As for those whose

parents and grandparents before them had been so fortunate as to keep their seats on the top, the conviction they cherished of the essential difference between their sort of humanity and the common article was absolute. The effect of such a delusion in moderating fellow feeling for the sufferings of the mass of men into a distant and philosophical compassion is obvious.[19]

Faced with fellow citizens, the well-off people in a market-foremost democracy presume that those others are suited to drudgery. "Let them do it," they may think. "If they don't like it, let them take personal responsibility for bettering themselves."

Such a dismissive attitude undermines democracy. The result is that we no longer think of "those people" as equals who have an equal right to contribute to democratic life, but as servants. How can democracy survive if some citizens view others as fundamentally incompetent, or as people of whom to take advantage?

We don't have to be trapped in this vicious circle. We can shift our value priorities. Just as market-foremost democracy has come into and gone out of prominence in different historical periods in the United States, maybe it is time to reorient our society. We can ask people to reconsider their values, provide greater support for institutions that promote democratic care, and make democracy more caring. It's time to set the Reagan Revolution aside for a Caring Revolution. Here's how to do it.

Making the Caring-With
Revolution Happen

J ust as the Reagan Revolution required a change in the nature of democratic life and in the nature of democratic
citizens, a caring revolution will require similar changes. As
citizens in a caring democracy, we would need to change not
only the discourse about care, not only our own daily concerns with care, but political and social institutions to make
them more caring as well.

Rethinking Responsibilities by
Caring about Care

A s I showed earlier, democratic caring means, in part,
assuring that everyone has an equal voice in deciding
how care duties are allocated. This is not as easy as it sounds.
We have become adept at understanding ourselves as workers and as consumers. Everyday economic life absorbs much

of our energy. Although we are also caring all the time, we don't usually think of caring as a central concern.

So our first change in moving toward a caring democracy is to start caring about care. We have to think differently about how we value the time we spend caring, and that means first noticing it as time we're spending doing worthwhile activities. As we move in this direction, those who haven't done their fair share of caring will erect a number of defenses to keep things the way they are.

Suppose we could get everyone to sit down around a table and discuss what caring responsibilities everyone should take. At first, we might think that the outcome would be a discussion resulting in some allocations for equal caring responsibilities, averaged out over a lifetime. In fact, we might instead hear a number of strident arguments that are made, explicitly or implicitly, that constitute excuses for why some people are already doing their fair share of caring— even when they really aren't. For one reason or another, they believe that they are privileged in their social standing and should therefore be free from caring responsibilities. Spiderman's Uncle Ben famously told him, "With great power comes great responsibility." But that's what uncles say to superheroes in the movies. In real life, with great power comes privileged irresponsibility.

Let's investigate some of these "passes" out of caring responsibilities so that we can preempt them and suggest more democratic ways to care. And let's notice ourselves using these passes, and stop giving ourselves excuses from meeting our own broad caring responsibilities.

"I'm No Good at Caring"

One way to get out of caring is to claim incompetence. We have heard these arguments before: "Women are naturally better at caring." "Some people are just better at care, and I'm not good at it." Indeed, the current framing of how we care now still rests upon the presupposition that care mainly occurs in the family, and that within the family, women are "naturally" better caregivers than men. Never mind that more and more men are doing caring work, especially for elder relatives. Even these men, though, still believe that women are better at the job.[20]

There is an obvious answer to this objection. Women and servants seem to be "naturals" at caregiving because those are the roles they have been expected to play. But the truth is, caring requires practice. People who are not good at caring now can become better at it by doing more of it. If we wish to live in a caring democracy, each of us has to become better at caring. And the best way to do that is to care *more*: being more attentive to others' needs, more willing to recognize and take on responsibilities, more competent and proud of the good caring that we do, and more willing to responsively adjust our caring depending upon how well its recipients receive it.

"I'm Busy Working"

Because care takes time, and people are often busy at work, it seems legitimate to claim that one's economic contribution is too important to delay by spending time on care. Similarly, up to the mid-nineteenth century, men who were drafted were able to send another body to do their military service.[21] The problem with this solution, though, is that it stigmatizes caring as an inferior sort of duty.

A "caring-with" alternative would require everyone to work less or spend a certain amount of time every day caring.[22] Of course, to really effect this change would require us to revolutionize how we think about our time, the place of work in our lives, and how we are compensated for our labor. Many workers now feel a 24/7 obligation to their jobs and end up answering emails from home and checking on the status of projects halfway around the world in the middle of the night. It would make considerably more sense for us to decide as a society that no one should put such work so completely above needs for care.

"I'm Taking Care of My Own Family"

I have already discussed how vicious circles of unequal care result from this attitude. There is a lot to be said for maintaining for one's own domestic world, but the culture of care that incites competitive parenting is not, in the end, very caring.

In a "caring-with" democracy, we would not be so desperate to seize every advantage over everyone else. Being greedy and defensive is exhausting. Being able to slow down a bit will allow us to realize that we can also be concerned about others without its taking a toll on care duties within our own family.

"Bootstraps Worked for Me—and Will for You"

The problem with this argument is that it's often untrue. Though we've all heard stories about self-made millionaires, most Americans end up in the same economic situation as their parents; and despite what we like to think, America provides less mobility than European countries.[23]

There are other dangers in taking the bootstraps argument too far. Many successful people got where they are more through good luck than hard work. To what extent do we want people to become risk-takers? There is some advantage in risk-taking, but if we perpetuate a conventional wisdom that says gambling is the only way to get ahead, people will engage in the kind of actions that led to the housing bubble in the late 2000s.

Bootstraps aside, is wealth what we want? Many people who engage in caring activities already know that caring, not money, lends meaning to life. Living as we do, constantly anxious about our status in an unforgiving economic order, makes us less capable of caring well. We think of wealth as another way to care. But suppose we could adjust our political institutions to support a different culture. Suppose we could live in a culture of care where we can reliably expect to be cared for when we find ourselves—and our loved ones—in need. Thinking about reallocating caring responsibilities is a start: but we need to go from thinking about changing care to actually changing the Politics *and* politics of care.

The Care-Foremost Citizen

After reflecting on the meaning and distribution of care responsibilities, we then need to devote ourselves to caring in democratic ways. Practice, practice, practice. We need to change both institutions and ourselves, but we can begin with changing our own lives.

Let's start close to home. What changes are necessary to live our daily lives in a more caring way? We may not be able to make all of these changes ourselves. If we go through the exercise of imagining how to change the amount of caring we actually do, some insights about "caring with" others will come to us. How is care distributed in your household? Is it fair? Is it just? What obstacles are there to caring better?

Next, let's think about institutions close to home. How caring is your workplace? Your school? Your place of worship? Your clubs? How can they be made more caring? To some extent, we can make changes within institutions near to us, and in other ways, we will come to recognize larger social and political institutional barriers to our better caring.

A number of sticking points will arise when we try to enact such changes. First, democratic care will require pluralism. People need to be able to care and be cared for in the ways that they want. Recall how broad the world of care is. There are many types of care across one's life.

Second, democratic care requires switching perspectives and not just thinking about what *we* want. We need also to look at care from the standpoint of care-receivers, who will have different ideas about what kind of care they want or need to receive. Should elderly people be sent to nursing homes, or should their families receive benefits to keep them at home? Some people will prefer one alternative, and others will prefer the other. In a "caring-with" democracy, we can set a goal of structuring institutions and practices so that each person's individual preferences can be honored.

Third, we need to recognize the diversity and ubiquity of different caring needs. It is easy to slip into the assumption that because some are more "needy" than others, they are less-worthwhile citizens. Neediness is not a natural thing: There is a "politics of needs interpretation" that makes some needs politically disabling compared to others. For citizens negotiating caring responsibilities, it will be necessary to be much more attentive to real needs and to allow people as much self-care as possible in order to preserve and enhance their roles as democratic citizens.

Fourth, we need to recognize that care is complex and that we aren't always the heroic caregiver in all the care stories we tell. Care does not happen, despite the familiar pictures in our heads, one-on-one between a single powerful caregiver and a single needy care-receiver. This kind of dyad gives rise to a frightening, seemingly inevitable, outcome of domination. In everyday reality, we negotiate caring needs, responsibilities, caregiving, and care-receiving in many directions at once. Once we begin to think about caregivers and care-receivers in more complex relationships, we can easily break down any lingering assumptions that care is necessarily hierarchical.

Democratic Caring Is Better Caring

If we are able to think more about caring democratically, not only will our democracy become more caring, but it will also become better at caring. Modeling care practices from a democratic standpoint has another benefit, as well. Flattening out hierarchies provides better opportunities for teams to work together, and thus a higher quality of care. A democratic, rather than top-down, organization of care work is more likely to produce the right solution to the right problem. Julie White's study of after-school programs in New York City in the 1990s gave an example of this practice at work. When experts decided what should be taught in the after-school programs, attendance was sporadic. When the parents were involved in determining the content of the program, many more children responded well.[24]

"Caring with" others, when we get good at it, produces the moral effects of trust and solidarity. In their work on the power of social capital, Harvard professor Robert Putnam and his colleagues discovered that only *trust* makes it possible for better information to flow through a social institution or network.[25] When sharp hierarchies of authority exist, as Putnam witnessed in southern Italy, those who are beholden to higher-ups in the social structure are more likely simply to tell the padrone what he wants to hear.

Lying might make a boss happy, but inaccurate information is less likely to produce good decisions. Less hierarchical authority patterns, such as were observed in other parts of Italy, were more likely to produce shared views, and those shared views were more likely to result in better action. Solidarity, as a social value, creates the conditions for caring among people and for greater responsiveness to democratic values.[26] Citizens who share a sense of common purpose with others are more likely to care for others and to feel committed to other citizens by virtue of their own caring acts. Furthermore, such solidarity creates a virtuous circle: since people are more attuned to others' needs, they are likely to be better at caring for them.

Finally, democracies would care better because they would require us to put many competing democratic values into the mix. We noted earlier that the allocation of caring responsibilities at present follows older patterns of exclusion, privileging some people's caring needs, and relegating the dirty work to others. In a way, this account of democracy— the allocation of caring responsibilities—allows us to return to the initial discussion that we had about the conflict between equality and freedom. There is no simple answer to the question: How will conflicting ideas about the allocation of care responsibilities work out? Some will assert that the democratic consensus has moved too far away from the freedom offered by the market mechanisms. Others will argue that some are still not doing their fair share of caring. These will be the stuff of ongoing democratic political disputes, and exactly the kind of conversation I hope to prompt with this essay.

A Caring Movement?

So, how do we get there? Political scientist Deborah Stone proposed in 2000 that we needed a "care movement."[27] She believed that if care-receivers, professional caregivers, and family members got together, they could make effective demands on the political system to reform how society allocates care and how care institutions are organized.

The argument I am making here is an even broader one. We need to stop trusting that "the market" will somehow magically meet all caring needs. Instead, democratic citizens need to care enough "about" care to start caring "for" care. We need to demand that caring responsibilities be reallocated in a way that is consistent with our other values, such as equality, justice, and freedom.

Once we start to see caring, we will see it everywhere: in the stories we tell about our lives, in the movies we watch, in the books we read, even in the disagreements we have with friends and family. We will demand that politicians stop talking about inconsequential matters and focus instead on how to improve our capacity to care for ourselves and others. This will not be a path free of serious disputes. But those are the disputes that should be at the heart of democratic politics.

As a democratic theorist, it's not my place to prescribe how people will effect this change. I am, however, confident that people have the ability to organize in their own best interests. We can understand the centrality of care within those interests and thereby make the world a safer, more caring, place.

The starting principle is this: We have got things backward now. The key to living well, for all people, is to live a care-filled life, a life in which one is cared for well by others when one needs it, cares well for oneself, and has room to provide for the care of other people, animals, institutions, and ideals that give one's life its particular meaning. A truly free society makes people free to care. A truly equal society gives people equal chances to be well cared for, and to engage in caring relationships. A truly just society does not use the market to hide current and past injustices. The purpose of economic life is to support care, not the other way around. Production is not an end in itself; it is a means to the end of living as well as we can. And in a democratic society, this means everyone can live well—not just the few.

These simple principles are easier to state than to imagine in practice, and they are simpler to imagine than to implement. It will be no simple task to turn society around, but I'll sketch in some dimensions of the task ahead.

Where to Begin

We must begin by making care a central value in our political world. We need to recognize the democratic ends of our caring practices. We should think about the diversity of caring needs and practices in our society and try to create social institutions congruent with that diversity.

Those seeking such a change will find an unlikely ally—the market. Markets produce new goods to meet new demands. Using markets to provide a myriad of ways, for example, to organize care for the elderly will make it more likely that each citizen finds suitable care. Flexibility is essential. Beyond using the market, though, to provide different possibilities, citizens also need to look closely at how well existing caring institutions—nursing homes, schools, mental health providers, and so forth—do their work. Once we begin to look at our own caring practices, we usually realize that we can do better. So, too, we can ask of existing and new institutions: Are there better ways for them to care? Evaluating how well society meets its caring responsibilities is not a one-time action. As a reiterative process in which citizens monitor and revisit their decisions, we can expect that, just as people become more adept at caring once they have become attentive to needs, citizens will become more adept at thinking about the consequences of their collective actions and decisions.

Because government will be closer to the issues that motivate and concern real citizens every day, the gap between government and citizens will diminish. As citizens with different views struggle to express themselves, no one will be the winner. As politics comes closer to the bone, and as the stakes become clearer, citizens will be able to appreciate their interdependence even as they pursue their own interests. Rethinking democracy as a system to support people as they try to live more humane and caring lives is the next step in our ongoing democratic revolution. Let's begin. Now.

Notes

1   Berenice Fisher and Joan C. Tronto, "Toward a Feminist Theory of Caring," in *Circles of Care*, ed. Emily K. Abel and Margaret Nelson (Albany, NY: SUNY Press, 1990), 40; Joan C. Tronto, *Moral Boundaries: A Political Argument for an Ethic of Care* (New York: Routledge, 1993), 103.

2   Nancy Fraser and Linda Gordon, "A Genealogy of Dependency: Tracing a Keyword of the U.S. Welfare State," *Signs* 19, no. 2 (1994).

3   Many paid care workers earn very low wages and have to rely on public assistance, as well. See Paraprofessional Healthcare Institute, "Paying the Price: How Poverty Wages Undermine Home Care in America" (Washington, D.C., 2015).

4   Aristotle, *Politics* II.ii.15.

5   Yet "partial citizenship" still characterizes the ways in which non-citizen, migrant caregivers are treated. See Rhacel Salazar Parreñas, *Servants of Globalization: Women, Migration, and Domestic Work* (Stanford, CA: Stanford University Press, 2001).

6   For a longer discussion and justification for this account of caring democracy, see Joan C. Tronto, *Caring Democracy: Markets, Equality and Justice* (New York: NYU Press, 2013).

7   Amy Bridges, "The Other Side of the Paycheck," in *Capitalist Patriarchy and the Case for Socialist Feminism*, ed. Zillah Eisenstein (New York: Monthly Review Press, 1979).

8   The family wage was not an uncontroversial solution to the problem of inadequate wages. For one recounting of this debate, see Nancy Fraser, "After the Family Wage: A Postindustrial Thought Experiment," in *Justice Interruptus: Critical Reflections on the "Postsocialist" Condition* (New York: Routledge, 1997).

9   Mignon Duffy, *Making Care Count: A Century of Gender, Race, and Paid Care Work* (New Brunswick, NJ: Rutgers University Press, 2011).

10   "Not only is the human being configured exhaustively as homo oeconomicus, but all dimensions of human life are cast in terms of a market rationality. . . . [It results in] the production of all human and institutional action as rational entrepreneurial action, conducted according to a calculus of utility, benefit, or satisfaction against a microeconomic grid of scarcity, supply and demand, and moral value-neutrality. Neoliberalism does not simply assume that all aspects of social, cultural, and political life can be reduced to such a calculus; rather, it develops institutional practices and rewards for enacting this vision." Wendy Brown, *Edgework: Critical Essays on Knowledge and Politics* (Princeton, NJ: Princeton University Press, 2005), 40.

11   Thomas L. Friedman, *The World Is Flat: A Brief History of the Globalized World in the Twenty-First Century* (New York: Allen Lane, 2005).

12   "It is true that if you never give kids responsibilities, they will take longer to become responsible. But there are some things that we are never taught at home. Thank you, school, for teaching me how to

find the volume of my cup of coffee. What I really needed to know was how to balance a checkbook, how to treat an open wound or even how to do taxes." Nick Gionet, "Young Writers: Maybe We're Spoiled, but Don't Criticize until We've Grown Up," *Star-Tribune*, May 28, 2015.

13 Juliet Schor, ed. *Do Americans Shop Too Much?* (Boston: Beacon, 2000); Juliet B. Schor, *The Overspent American* (New York: HarperCollins, 1998); Juliet B. Schor, *Born to Buy* (New York: Scribner, 2004).

14 Robert H. Frank, *Luxury Fever: Money and Happiness in an Era of Excess* (Princeton, NJ: Princeton University Press, 2000).

15 George W. Bush, "First Inaugural Address" (bartleby.com, 2001).

16 A. Fernald and A. Weisleder, "Twenty Years after 'Meaningful Differences,' It's Time to Reframe the 'Deficit' Debate about the Importance of Children's Early Language Experience," *Human Development* 58, no. 1 (2015): 1.

17 See Randy Albelda, Mignon Duffy, and Nancy Folbre, "Counting on Care Work: Human Infrastructure in Massachusetts" (Amherst: University of Massachusetts, 2009).

18 Arlie Russell Hochschild, *The Time Bind: When Work Becomes Home and Home Becomes Work*, 1st ed. (New York: Metropolitan Books, 1997), xii–xiii.

19 Edward Bellamy, *Looking Backward, 2000–1887* (Boston: Ticknor and Co., 1888): 16–17.

20 Lori D. Campbell and Michael P. Carroll, "The Incomplete Revolution," *Men & Masculinities* 9 (2007).

21 See, e.g., Thomas Hobbes, *Leviathan*, chapter 21 section 16.

22 I am grateful for conversations with Jennifer Nedelsky about this question.

23 That increasing levels of economic inequality are seriously undermining equality of opportunity, see Joseph E. Stiglitz, *The*

43

Price of Inequality: How Today's Divided Society Endangers Our Future (New York: Norton, 2013), 22–25.

24 Julie Anne White, *Democracy, Justice and the Welfare State: Reconstructing Public Care* (University Park: Penn State University Press, 2000).

25 Robert D. Putnam, *Making Democracy Work: Civic Traditions in Modern Italy* (Princeton NJ: Princeton University Press, 1993).

26 Carol Gould, "Varieties of Global Responsibility: Social Connection, Human Rights, and Transnational Solidarity," in *Dancing with Iris: The Philosophy of Iris Marion Young*, ed. Anne Ferguson and Mechthild Nagel (New York: Oxford, 2009); Joseph M. Schwartz, *The Future of Democratic Equality: Rebuilding Social Solidarity in a Fragmented America* (New York: Routledge, 2009); Selma L. Sevenhuijsen, *Citizenship and the Ethics of Care* (London: Routledge, 1998).

27 Deborah Stone, "Why We Need a Care Movement," *The Nation*, March 13 2000.

Bibliography

Albelda, Randy, Mignon Duffy, and Nancy Folbre. "Counting on Care Work: Human Infrastructure in Massachusetts." Amherst: University of Massachusetts, 2009.

Bellamy, Edward. *Looking Backward, 2000–1887.* 1888.

Bridges, Amy. "The Other Side of the Paycheck." In *Capitalist Patriarchy and the Case for Socialist Feminism*, edited by Zillah Eisenstein. New York: Monthly Review Press, 1979.

Brown, Wendy. *Edgework: Critical Essays on Knowledge and Politics.* Princeton, NJ: Princeton University Press, 2005.

Bush, George W. "First Inaugural Address." bartleby.com, 2001.

Campbell, Lori D., and Michael P. Carroll. "The Incomplete Revolution." *Men & Masculinities* 9 (2007): 491–508.

Duffy, Mignon. *Making Care Count: A Century of Gender, Race, and Paid Care Work.* New Brunswick, NJ: Rutgers University Press, 2011.

Fernald, A., and A. Weisleder. "Twenty Years after 'Meaningful Differences,' It's Time to Reframe the 'Deficit' Debate about the Importance of Children's Early Language Experience." *Human Development* 58, no. 1 (2015): 1–4.

Fisher, Berenice, and Joan C. Tronto. "Toward a Feminist Theory of Caring." In *Circles of Care*, edited by Emily K. Abel and Margaret Nelson, 36–54. Albany, NY: SUNY Press, 1990.

Frank, Robert H. *Luxury Fever: Money and Happiness in an Era of Excess*. Princeton, NJ: Princeton University Press, 2000.

Fraser, Nancy. "After the Family Wage: A Postindustrial Thought Experiment." In *Justice Interruptus: Critical Reflections on the "Postsocialist" Condition*. New York: Routledge, 1997.

Fraser, Nancy, and Linda Gordon. "A Genealogy of Dependency: Tracing a Keyword of the U.S. Welfare State." *Signs* 19, no. 2 (1994): 309–36.

Friedman, Thomas L. *The World Is Flat: A Brief History of the Globalized World in the Twenty-First Century*. New York: Allen Lane, 2005.

Gionet, Nick. "Young Writers: Maybe We're Spoiled, but Don't Criticize until We've Grown Up." *Star-Tribune*, May 28, 2015.

Gould, Carol. "Varieties of Global Responsibility: Social Connection, Human Rights, and Transnational Solidarity." *In Dancing with Iris: The Philosophy of Iris Marion Young*, edited by Anne Ferguson and Mechthild Nagel, 199–211. New York: Oxford, 2009.

Hochschild, Arlie Russell. *The Time Bind: When Work Becomes Home and Home Becomes Work*. 1st ed. New York: Metropolitan Books, 1997.

Paraprofessional Healthcare Institute. "Paying the Price: How Poverty Wages Undermine Home Care in America." Washington, D.C., 2015.

Parreñas, Rhacel Salazar. *Servants of Globalization: Women, Migration, and Domestic Work*. Stanford, CA: Stanford University Press, 2001.

Putnam, Robert D. *Making Democracy Work: Civic Traditions in Modern Italy*. Princeton NJ: Princeton University Press, 1993.

Schor, Juliet B. *Born to Buy*. New York: Scribner, 2004.

——, ed. *Do Americans Shop Too Much?* Boston: Beacon, 2000.

——. *The Overspent American*. New York: HarperCollins, 1998.

Schwartz, Joseph M. *The Future of Democratic Equality: Rebuilding Social Solidarity in a Fragmented America*. New York: Routledge, 2009.

Sevenhuijsen, Selma L. *Citizenship and the Ethics of Care*. London: Routledge, 1998.

Stiglitz, Joseph E. *The Price of Inequality: How Today's Divided Society Endangers Our Future*. New York: Norton, 2013.

Stone, Deborah. "Why We Need a Care Movement." *The Nation*, March 13, 2000, 13–15.

Tronto, Joan C. *Caring Democracy: Markets, Equality, and Justice*. New York: NYU Press, 2013.

——. *Moral Boundaries: A Political Argument for an Ethic of Care*. New York: Routledge, 1993.

White, Julie Anne. *Democracy, Justice and the Welfare State: Reconstructing Public Care*. University Park: Penn State University Press, 2000.

About the Author

Joan C. Tronto is professor of political science at the University of Minnesota, Twin Cities. She previously taught at Bowdoin College and at Hunter College and the Graduate Center, City University of New York; she was also a Fulbright Fellow in Bologna, Italy. She is the author of several books: *Moral Boundaries: A Political Argument for an Ethic of Care* (Routledge, 1993), *Le risque ou le care* (Presses Universitaires de France, 2012), and *Caring Democracy: Markets, Equality, and Justice* (NYU Press, 2013). She has also published numerous articles about care and its place in contemporary national and global politics. Her work has been translated into seven other languages.